THE ORIGIN AND TRANSMISSION
OF THE NEW TESTAMENT

THE ORIGIN
AND TRANSMISSION
OF THE NEW TESTAMENT

A SHORT INTRODUCTION

L. D. TWILLEY
B.D.

Wm. B. Eerdmans Publishing Company
Grand Rapids, Michigan

First Published . . . 1957
Reprinted 1959

Published in Britain by Oliver & Boyd

PHOTOLITHOPRINTED BY CUSHING - MALLOY, INC.
ANN ARBOR, MICHIGAN, UNITED STATES OF AMERICA

To the memory of

Dr. P. W. EVANS

devout scholar
revered principal
honoured friend

PREFACE

THE PURPOSE OF THIS BOOK is twofold. First, to give
a brief outline of the early days of the Church as
portrayed in the New Testament, and to indicate
within that history the points at which the various
New Testament books were written; secondly, to show
how these books have been transmitted through the
centuries down to our own day.

As regards the dating of some of the books there is
much diversity of opinion. In the main body of the
work will be found the dating favoured by the author,
but the main alternative dates will be indicated in
paragraphs set in smaller type. It is suggested that
these paragraphs should be omitted on first reading,
so that a clear, straightforward account will be presented to the reader. If the book is then re-read in its
entirety, the critical points will be appreciated much
more fully.

It is obvious that in a work which tries to embrace
such a wide field within such a small compass, the
arguments for various dates can only be most briefly
suggested, and many points of great importance only
touched upon lightly. The book will, however, have
served its purpose, if it helps towards a clearer understanding of the circumstances behind the writing and
transmission of the New Testament books, and leads
the reader to larger and far more adequate works.

The Scripture quotations are mostly from the Revised Version.

My thanks are due to Dr Beasley-Murray, M.A., B.D., M.TH., to my wife, for help given during the preparation of the manuscript, and also to the publishers.

L. D. T.

CONTENTS

CHAPTER I

THE CHURCH IN PALESTINE

ASTOUNDING news! The Messiah has come! That was
the message the early Christians gave to the world.
We hear it first from the lips of Peter on the day of 30[1]
Pentecost, and its echo resounds all through the New
Testament. Peter's words are recorded in *Acts* II.36:
"God hath made him both Lord and Christ [i.e.
Messiah], this Jesus whom ye crucified." Here then
is the very heart of the Christian message or Gospel—
Jesus is the Messiah, the very Sent-one of God. If we
analyse Peter's four sermons recorded in the opening
chapters of *Acts* we find that they are really an ampli-
fication of this theme. Professor C. H. Dodd in *The
Apostolic Preaching and its Developments*[2] does this
and discovers six main points in the primitive Gospel.
First, the Age of Fulfilment has dawned: *Acts* II.16,
III.18 ("The things which God foreshadowed by the
mouth of all the prophets . . . he thus fulfilled").
Secondly, this has taken place through the ministry,
death, and resurrection of Jesus. Here we have the
historical basis of the message, and it is particularly
evident in *Acts* II (of which vss. 30, 31 refer to Christ's
Davidic descent; 22 to His ministry; and 24–31 to
His resurrection). Thirdly, Jesus has been exalted

---

[1] All dates given in the margin are A.D.
[2] Hodder and Stoughton, London 1944.

at God's right hand: *Acts* II.33 ("Being therefore by the right hand of God exalted"), III.13, v.31. Fourthly, the Holy Spirit in the Church is a sign of Christ's present power and glory: *Acts* II.33 ("Having received of the Father the promise of the Holy Spirit, he hath poured forth this which ye see and hear"). Fifthly, the Messianic Age will reach its consummation in the return of Christ: *Acts* III.21 ("[Jesus], whom the heavens must receive until the time of restoration of all things.") Sixthly, an appeal for repentance and offer of forgiveness and of the Holy Spirit forms the conclusion: *Acts* II.38 ("Repent ye and be baptised every one of you in the name of Jesus Christ unto the remission of sins; and ye shall receive the gift of the Holy Spirit"), III.19, IV.12, v.31. Now, it must be borne in mind that this is not the gospel of Peter, but The Gospel, the common possession of the early Church, and it can be traced in Paul and the other New Testament writers. It is true that there are minor variations and differences of emphasis, but in its essentials it is the same for all.

How did the Jews react to this message? For generations they had impatiently awaited the coming of the Messiah, and now the great day had arrived. Yet it would hardly be true to say that their hopes had now been realised, for the Sent-one of God was not the Messiah of their dreams. The manner of His coming was not as many had expected, and alas! multitudes of His own people had derided Him, rejected Him, and finally engineered His death. Confronted by the bold declaration that "Jesus is the Messiah," their natural reaction was, "Give us the proof!" Their own preconceived ideas regarding the Messiah could not easily be placed on one side as they listened to the fervent preaching of the Christian evangelists. How could the Old Testament teaching on the Christ—the Messiah—be reconciled with the life and work of the Carpenter of Nazareth? That was a problem which the earliest preachers had to face. They were making great claims for Jesus, and there was only one way to substantiate them—by showing from passages and texts in the Old Testament that the details of Jesus' life had been foretold within its pages. Thus arose the use, by early preachers, of so-called "proof-texts" or "*testimonia*." These verified the Gospel facts. 30-40

A glance at Peter's sermon on the day of Pentecost in *Acts* II will reveal the method. Peter wishes to show that Christ's resurrection was in the divine plan of things; he does this by appealing to *Ps.* XVI.10 ("For thou wilt not leave my soul to Sheol; neither wilt thou suffer thine holy one to see corruption"; *cf. Acts* II.27). Also the exaltation of Jesus was foretold in the Old Testament, as is clear from *Ps.* CX.1 ("The Lord said unto my lord, sit thou at my right hand until I make thine enemies thy footstool"); this verse is quoted by Peter in *Acts* II.34 f. Written lists of these *testimonia* were soon in circulation and were used freely by preachers and writers. Some parts of the Old Testament (*e.g. Is., Pss.*) were particularly valuable in this respect. We find Paul addressing the Jews at Antioch quoting *Ps.* XVI.10 to substantiate the fact of the Resurrection; Peter the writer (*I Pet.* II.6) quotes *Is.* XXVIII.16 ("Behold, I lay in Zion for a foundation a stone, a tried stone, a precious corner stone of sure foundation"), to substantiate the Christian statement that Christ is the chief corner-stone of the Church.

When the evangelists wrote their *Gospels*, proof-texts were freely incorporated into the narrative of their works. Mark, for example, right at the beginning of his *Gospel* (*Mk.* 1.2), quotes *Mal.* III.1 to show how God had spoken beforehand of the preparatory work of John the Baptist. Matthew in particular made great use of the Old Testament in writing his *Gospel*. Swete says[1] that there are 46 distinct Old Testament quotations in the Synoptic Gospels (*i.e.* the first three), of which 40 are found in Matthew's. Out of this 40, 18 are found in his *Gospel* only, and not in the other two. Of course many of these texts are merely quotations from the Old Testament, but others are mentioned by the evangelist to substantiate the facts he gives and to reveal the divine purpose behind our Lord's life. For example, the thirty pieces of silver are shown (*Mt.* XXVII.9) to have been foretold by Jeremiah. There can be no doubt that these proof-texts carried a good deal of conviction to the Jewish readers. Later on, in the third century, we find Cyprian in Africa using *testimonia*, and to this day the exponent of the New Testament often uses the Old Testament to elucidate its message.

These proof-texts must have been collected at an early date, and it would be natural to assume that the collection, being made in Palestine by Jews, would exist in Aramaic, the vernacular language of Palestine at the time of our Lord. The fact that some of the Old

---

[1] *Introduction to the Old Testament in Greek* (1914), p. 391.

Testament quotations found only in Matthew's *Gospel* and not in the others differ from both the Hebrew Old Testament and the Greek version of the Old Testament (the Septuagint) seems to support this assumption. Their slight divergence in wording might be explained on the basis that they were being quoted from an Aramaic list, but some scholars (*e.g.* Professor F. C. Burkitt) explain their difference from our Hebrew Old Testament by assuming that the compiler of the list of proof-texts used a Hebrew Bible differing slightly from our own.

In *Mk.* 1.2, there appears to be a mistake which is best accounted for on the assumption that Mark was using *testimonia*. The best manuscripts read, "Even as it is written in Isaiah the prophet, Behold I send . . ."; and this is the reading followed in the Revised Version. The words quoted by Mark, however, are not *all* from Isaiah, the first part of the quotation being from *Mal.* III.1, and the second from *Is.* XL.3. It appears likely that these two quotations were together in a list of proof-texts, and that the page was headed by the name "Isaiah," with the result that Mark quoted them both as being from the hand of that prophet. In a similar way, the early Father Irenaeus quotes in one place from Micah and Amos under the one heading of Amos (Swete, *Mark*, p. 2).

So much for the *testimonia* with their apologetic appeal. As new converts were made and Churches formed, the need was felt for sayings of the Master to be passed on to the new disciples for the guidance of their daily lives. A list of such sayings was used by Matthew and Luke in the composition of their *Gospels* 50 and is usually denoted by the letter *Q* (the initial letter of the German word *Quelle*, "source"). If the three Synoptic Gospels are set out in parallel columns, it will be found that Matthew's and Luke's both contain a large part of Mark's, but there is some material which they both have in common which was not derived from it. As the very close verbal resemblances indicate, this matter which is common to Matthew's and Luke's *Gospels* but not Mark is clearly derived from some written source, and it consists mainly of sayings of the Master. Now though it is quite clear that, as used by Matthew and Luke, this "sayings document" (*Q*) must have been in Greek, it is probable that like the *testimonia* it originally existed in Aramaic. Papias (second century) states that "Matthew composed the oracles (λόγια) in the Hebrew language (*i.e.* Aramaic), and each one interpreted them as he could." What does Papias mean by λόγια? Some have contended that he refers to a gospel, but many have thought he means *testimonia*, especially as Matthew incorporates so many proof-texts. It is possible, however, that the reference is to the sayings document *Q*, especially as this is one of the sources behind the *Gospel according to St Matthew*. One thing is certain, however; the *Gospel according to St Matthew*, as we have it, is not a translation from a Hebrew or Aramaic original.

There are *logia* or "sayings of our Lord" in other books of the New Testament besides the Gospels. Paul's quotation of Christ's words "It is more blessed to give than to receive" (*Acts* xx.35) must have come from some such list. The reader will notice that this saying is not found in our *Gospels*. Although James does not definitely say so, when he says "Swear not either by the heaven or by the earth" (*James* v.12), he might be quoting from a sayings documents later incorporated in *Mt.* v.34.[1]

During these early days of the Church there were many who had hallowed memories not only of the Master's words but also of his gracious acts. These 30-65 memories would be shared with others and thus a body of *oral tradition* would be built up in addition to the written tradition mentioned above. Stories about Jesus, parables, and miracles would be retold by those who had heard and witnessed them. In the course of constant re-telling, these would gradually assume a fairly fixed form in the Christian community. In recent years it has been the task of form criticism to investigate what was happening in this oral period, and to classify according to form the material that lies behind our written *Gospels*.

It seems surprising to us to-day that full written accounts of our Lord's words and deeds were so long delayed; but while the great leaders of the Church were still alive, the need to write was not pressing. People could go to them for confirmation of the facts, and the living voice was to them far more valuable and authentic than the written word. Besides this, the early Church expected the speedy return of Christ; why waste time writing? Preaching was the great priority. It was

[1] Much interest was aroused when, in 1897, B. P. Grenfell and A. S. Hunt discovered at Oxyrhyncus a page from a third-century collection of sayings of our Lord. On this papyrus sheet there were eight sayings, most of them differing greatly from anything in the canonical *Gospels*. Six years later, the same scholars discovered another sheet, of about the same date, which contained five more uncanonical sayings.

only as time passed and the Apostles died or were martyred, and the second advent was delayed, that the need for written accounts became urgent.

We have reviewed in this chapter the earliest evidence for the life and teaching of Jesus: the *testimonia*; Q and possibly other lists of sayings; and oral tradition. We shall see later how this material was incorporated into our *Gospels*, but we must always bear in mind that behind the four *Gospels* and entrusted to the early Church there lay The Gospel, the κήρυγμα (kērygma) or proclamation of the act of God in sending Jesus into the world. The four *Gospels* enshrine The Gospel in its written form, but The Gospel in all its fulness is only found by contact with the living Christ; ultimately He is The Gospel.

Let us now look at the expanding Church and see the documents which arose in the course of its forward movement.

CHAPTER II

THE CHURCH EXPANDS

LUKE tells us that one of the last commands of the risen Jesus to His disciples was to tarry in Jerusalem until they were endued with power from on high. Thus they abode in the city, and ten days after Jesus had ascended the Holy Spirit came upon them empowering them for their universal mission. It was only natural that Jerusalem should become the headquarters of the work in Palestine; and James—the Lord's brother—was appointed head of the Church in Jerusalem.

The first seven chapters of *Acts* deal with this Church and the consolidation of the work there, but soon severe persecution struck the Church and in *Acts* VIII.1 we read that the Christians at Jerusalem were all scattered abroad except for the Apostles. This persecution was greatly used of God for the spreading of the Gospel, however, for soon we hear of the word being preached in Samaria, Damascus, Caesarea and Antioch, all important towns in the country.

In those early days, the lot of these scattered Christian communities was far from easy, and there was need for encouragement besides guidance in their struggles. James saw the need for this and wrote a short tract on the Christian's outlook and way of life. We call it the *Epistle of James*.[1] With its strong 46

[1] But see below, p. 28.

ethical and practical appeal, this tract is just what we would expect from this Jewish-Christian who had so recently left the fold of Judaism.

But the message of salvation could not be confined to one race and soon the promptings of the Spirit were felt in the Church at Antioch in Syria. "Separate me

MAP 1
Paul's Missionary Journeys

Barnabas and Saul for the work whereunto I have called them" (*Acts* XIII.2). There was nothing to do but obey, and so the Church solemnly set apart these two ambassadors of Christ for the wider ministry— the ministry to the Gentiles.

47 PAUL and Barnabas took John Mark with them and sailed to Cyprus. After some missionary work in that country they journeyed on to Asia Minor, landing at

Perga. For some reason John Mark left them here and went back home, but Paul and his companion Barnabas pushed inland to Antioch (*Acts* XIII.14). The Christian message was warmly received by the Gentiles in this town, but the Jews became jealous and forced the Apostles to leave. The next town they visited was Iconium (*Acts* XIII.51), and here they stayed for some while and made a number of converts. Their work, however, was brought to an end by the threats of certain Jews and Gentiles that they would stone them, and so they moved on to Lystra (*Acts* XIV.6). Here Paul healed a cripple, and this had a profound effect on the inhabitants. Unfortunately, the work was interrupted by certain Jews from Antioch and Iconium who succeeded in stirring up the people against them, so that Paul was stoned. The two Apostles next called at Derbe, where many disciples were made (*Acts* XIV.20), and then retraced their steps through Lystra, Iconium and Antioch to Perga, from whence they sailed home to Antioch (*Acts* XIV.26).

Their return was an occasion of great excitement 48 for the Church at Antioch, and the Christians eagerly listened to the account of their journey and of the way in which large numbers of Gentiles had embraced the faith. The joy of these victories was over-shadowed, however, by the news that false teachers had already reached these new Churches in the Roman province of Galatia and were pressing upon the Gentiles there the necessity for circumcision. This was a serious challenge to the Apostle, as he had taught that salvation was by faith alone. He immediately wrote a letter to them (the *Epistle to the Galatians*) reminding

them of his own teaching.[1] This letter had hardly
been written when certain men arrived at Antioch from
Jerusalem who maintained the very point of view that

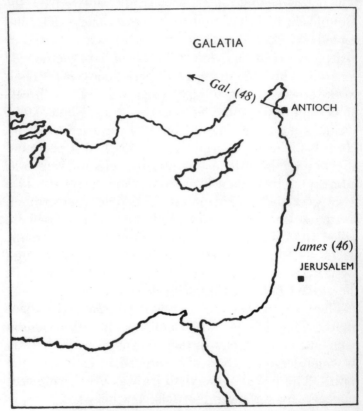

FIG. I: LETTERS WRITTEN PROBABLY BEFORE PAUL'S
SECOND JOURNEY

Paul was contesting against—the necessity for circumcision. Paul and Barnabas had a lively discussion
with them, and it soon became obvious that the whole

[1] But see below, p. 20.

question of the relationship between Judaism and Christianity needed to be looked into. The Church at Antioch accordingly decided (*Acts* xv.2) to ask Paul and Barnabas to go to Jerusalem with others from the Church to thrash this matter out with the Apostles and elders there.

This Council of Jerusalem, as it is called, was held 49 under the chairmanship of James the Lord's brother, and its discussions are given in *Acts* xv.6 ff. After careful deliberation it was agreed that a letter should be sent to the Gentiles telling them to abstain from things sacrificed to idols, and from blood, and from things strangled, and from fornication, but that no other legal demands would be made on them. We are told in *Acts* xv.21, that it was out of deference to the Jews that these requirements were made, but the point to be noted is that these demands were so few, and a moral victory had in fact been won for Gentile liberty.

After further time spent in Antioch, Paul suggested to Barnabas that they visit the new Gentile churches that they had founded. This was in order to strengthen them in the faith, and also, as appears from *Acts* xvi.4, to make known to them the decisions made at Jerusalem. Because Paul refused to take John Mark with them on this journey (on account of his having turned back at Perga on the previous journey), Barnabas would not accompany him, and Paul chose Silas as his companion. They journeyed by land through Derbe 49 and Lystra, and it was at this latter place that Timothy joined the missionaries. Under the guidance of the Spirit they made their way thence to Troas where probably Luke the physician was added to their company. (Luke uses "we" in *Acts* XVI.10–18, as though he were with them from Troas to Philippi.)

A strong church was established in Philippi (which lay just across the Aegean Sea from Troas)—a church which ever held a warm place in Paul's heart. Lydia (a seller of purple), a fortune-teller, and the Philippian gaoler, were notable converts in this Macedonian town. The party moved on to Thessalonica (*Acts* XVII.1), and although they only spent three weeks here, many accepted the faith before Paul was finally accused by the Jews, brought before the local rulers, and forced to move on to Beroea (*Acts* XVII.10). His work was once again interrupted by Jews and the brethren there thought it advisable to send him by sea to Athens, Silas and Timothy remaining in Beroea for the time being. Paul seems to have had little success in Athens, and moved on to Corinth (XVIII.1). Here he was joined by his two companions, Silas and Timothy, and together they laboured for a year and a half in this important town.

As a result of the report that Timothy and Silas gave about the Church in Thessalonica, Paul wrote his *First Epistle to the Thessalonians*. He was able to rejoice at their growth in Christian character and faithfulness under persecution, but found it necessary to defend himself against Jewish slanders that were current in Thessalonica, and also to give further teaching on morality. A particularly pressing problem to the Christians there appears to have been what would happen to those who had died by the time Christ came again. Paul comforts them with the thought that all Christians will share in the blessings of that day. Apparently Paul's letter was misunderstood as implying that the second advent was imminent, and Paul had to write another (his *Second Epistle to the Thessalonians*) to give further teaching on this 50 important subject.

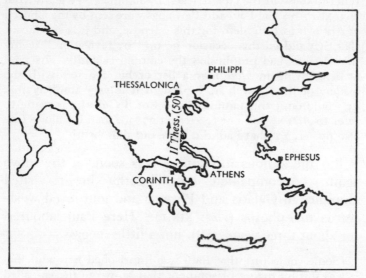

FIG. 2: LETTERS WRITTEN PROBABLY DURING PAUL'S SECOND JOURNEY

From Corinth Paul sailed with Priscilla and Aquila to Ephesus. Here he left his two companions, and continued his voyage alone to Caesarea, whence he went up to Jerusalem in order to keep the Passover. After the feast, he went to Antioch and remained there for some while (*Acts* XVIII.23).

[Some scholars hold that Paul wrote to the Galatians subsequent to the Council of Jerusalem and not before it,

as maintained above. They interpret *Gal.* II.2 ("I went up
[*i.e.* to Jerusalem] by revelation and I laid before them the
Gospel which I preach among the Gentiles but privately
before them of repute, lest by any means I should be running
or had run in vain"), as being a reference to that Council,
and accordingly have to date *Galatians* later. This verse
more likely refers to Paul's visit for the purpose of bringing
relief to those in the city stricken by famine. We learn from
Acts XI.27–30 that Paul and Barnabas were sent by the Church
at Antioch to Jerusalem for this purpose, and it is significant
that they did on this occasion go up "by revelation," seeing
that Agabus had prophesied the coming calamity. As Paul
is here giving in *Galatians* a list of his contacts with the
leaders of the Church in Jerusalem it is very unlikely that
he would omit this famine visit. But if *Gal.* II.2 is made to
refer to *Acts* XV and not to *Acts* XI.27–30, then it follows (see
also pp. 11, 20) that Paul did leave out that visit.]

52   But the zealous missionary was soon on the move
again.   Accompanied by Timothy he re-visited
churches in Galatia and Phrygia and journeyed westwards to Ephesus (*Acts* XIX.1). Here Paul laboured
for about three years, with not a little success.

[Some conjecture that Paul was imprisoned here and that
it was during this imprisonment that he wrote the so-called
"imprisonment epistles"—*Ephesians, Philippians, Colossians*,
and *Philemon*. Although *Acts* does not mention an imprisonment, it is not beyond the bounds of possibility, since Luke
the author does not give complete details of all that happened
to the Apostle. For example, Paul mentions "fighting with
beasts at Ephesus" (*I Cor.* XV.32)—which could conceivably
be literal—although Luke says nothing about this. Neither
are all the sufferings which Paul lists in *II Corinthians* given
in *Acts*. Various points, in *Philippians* especially, make the
possibility of that letter having been written from Ephesus
quite feasible. Paul tells the Philippians in that letter that
he hoped to visit them soon. This fits in well with his stay

at Ephesus, as he did in fact visit Philippi very shortly afterwards, whereas if the words were written during an imprisonment at Rome they are less natural. He also says in this letter that the Philippians had lacked an opportunity of sending him a gift. This could hardly be the case if he was writing from Rome over ten years after the founding of the church in that city (see below, p. 23.)]

During his stay here news reached Paul that forni- 53 cation was being practised at Corinth, and he wrote a letter dealing with the matter. This letter has not come down to us, but it is mentioned in *I Cor.* v.9 ("I wrote unto you in my epistle to have no company with fornicators") and is frequently referred to as the "previous epistle." Some scholars have thought that a fragment of it has survived in *II Cor.* VI.14–VII.1, but this on the whole seems unlikely.

A little later the Corinthian Christians sent a letter to Paul asking him various questions. These related particularly to marriage, idol-foods, the proper conduct of public worship and the Lord's Supper, spiritual gifts, the Resurrection of the dead, and the collection for poor believers. The letter was accompanied by certain of the family of Chloe, who told Paul that there were dissensions in the Church at Corinth. All these matters were dealt with by Paul in his reply—the letter that we know as *I Corinthians.* 54

The Church at Corinth was very immature in the faith, and soon more bad news reached the Apostle. Just what this was is not known, but Paul appears to have paid a visit to Corinth to put matters straight. This visit is not mentioned in *Acts*, but is implied by *II Cor.* XII.14 ("This is the third time I am ready to come to you") and by *II Cor.* XIII.1–2: according to *Acts*, the Apostle had only once been to Corinth before this. This visit is usually referred to as the "painful visit." (Some, however, contend that the verses in question only refer to a visit the Apostle intended to make, not to one that he actually made.) It appears from such verses as *II Cor.* II.5–11 and VII.12 that the Apostle was insulted on this occasion, and that on returning to Ephesus he wrote a severe letter, part of which may perhaps (but not probably) be found in *II Cor.* X–XIII.10. Paul was so worried by the distress that this severe letter might cause to the Corinthians that he hurried to Troas and on to Macedonia to meet Titus (who had delivered the severe letter), and to hear from him what effect it had had. Paul met Titus in Macedonia, and was overjoyed to hear that the disobedient Christian who had been causing so much trouble to the Corinthian Christians had been disowned and punished, and that the Corinthians were on friendly terms with Paul again. With great thanksgiving to God Paul wrote *II Corinthians* from Macedonia in the year 56 A.D.

56

[It should be noted that some reject the evidence for the "previous epistle" and the "severe letter." They make the words "I wrote" in *I Cor.* V.9 refer to *I Corinthians* itself, thus making that letter the "previous epistle." This is a possible interpretation of the Greek. On this theory, *II Corinthians* is made the "severe letter."]

Paul continued his journey through Greece as far as Corinth. Here he stayed for three months, during which time he wrote his *Epistle to the Romans*. Some

57

scholars have strongly contested the likelihood that Rome was the destination of this letter. This is partly due to the fact that the words "in Rome" (*Rom.* 1.7) are omitted in the ninth-century manuscript G and in the margin of the eleventh-century manuscript known as 1908. This is poor evidence on which to

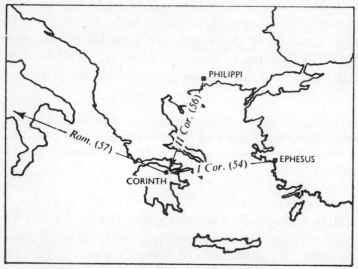

FIG. 3 : LETTERS WRITTEN PROBABLY DURING PAUL'S
THIRD JOURNEY

base such an important conclusion. The placing of the doxology in different places in the last three chapters by different manuscripts has also been held to go against the unity of the letter and against its Roman destination. It is said, too, that since he had never actually visited the Church at Rome, Paul is unlikely to have known all the people listed in *Rom.* XVI. These and various other points from both external and internal evidence have been raised, but in the author's opinion the best explanation of all the facts is that the epistle as we have it was written to the Roman Christians, and later modified and circulated as a treatise on doctrine to various churches. It was particularly suitable for instruction in the Christian faith because it deals so fully with the doctrine of salvation. Having shown the universal need of salvation, it goes on to explain that it can only be appropriated by faith. The new life thus obtained is described. The problem of God's apparent rejection of his chosen people, Israel, is then dealt with, and the epistle closes with various ethical instructions.

[Owing to the similarity of subject (*i.e.* justification by faith) in both *Romans* and *Galatians* some would place the writing of the latter here at Corinth, and not earlier (see above, p. 11).]

After his stay at Corinth, Paul journeyed to Philippi, and there kept the Passover (*Acts* xx.6). Thence he continued by sea to Troas and on to Miletus near Ephesus. Paul summoned the elders of the Church at Ephesus to meet him at Miletus and delivered a solemn address exhorting them to "shepherd the Church of God" (*Acts* xx.28). After a touching farewell, the Apostle resumed his voyage, and passing to the west of Cyprus eventually landed at Tyre (*Acts* xxi.3). The disciples here warned Paul not to proceed to Jerusalem with the gifts which he had collected from the churches for the poor Christians there, but the undaunted Apostle pressed on to Ptolemais and Caesarea. Here he abode for some while at the home of Philip the Evangelist.

CHAPTER III

THE CHURCH UNDER FIRE

DURING his stay with Philip the Evangelist at Caesarea, Paul received another warning not to go up to Jerusalem, this time from the prophet Agabus. But the Apostle's mind was made up, and he set out with Mnason for the capital city. Paul was warmly received 57 there by James, the head of the Jerusalem Church, and by the elders (*Acts* xxi.17). They were glad to hear of Paul's success among the Gentiles, but pointed out to him that many of the Jewish Christians were very disturbed by his teaching that circumcision and attention to Jewish customs were unimportant. They consequently persuaded him to show his deference for the Jewish Law by defraying the expenses of four Nazirites who had completed their vows. This Paul did, but towards the end of the allotted seven days certain Jews from Asia saw Paul in the Temple and stirred up the people against him. They eventually dragged him out of the Temple, and would have killed him, but for the intervention of Claudius Lysias, the Roman Commandant. Paul was taken into the barracks for safe custody, but was later permitted to speak to the people. On the following day Paul was formally accused by the chief priests, but this only resulted in a quarrel between the Pharisees and Sadducees. Seeing their hopes of getting Paul out of the way by legal means fading, certain of the reckless Jews vowed to kill him as he was being brought down for trial. News of this came to the ears of Lysias, however, and he decided to dispatch Paul secretly by night to Caesarea to Felix, the Governor (*Acts* XXIII.24). He wrote a letter to Felix explaining the situation. Felix heard Paul's case, but kept him in bonds, as he hoped to receive money for his release. His successor Festus also showed no sympathy, and Paul, despairing of ever getting justice outside Rome exercised his right as a Roman citizen, and appealed to Caesar (*Acts* XXV.12).

57-59   During Paul's two years' imprisonment at Caesarea, Luke seems to have been his companion. Now Luke had never seen or heard Jesus, and he was naturally interested in the oral tradition about Him that circulated around Caesarea. Luke decided to combine this material with what he had read in *Q* to form the framework of an account of the life of Jesus. This work is usually referred to as *Proto-Luke*, and it formed the basis of the Gospel that he wrote later in Rome.

Luke probably also obtained at this time much information from the Apostles and other early Christians about the early days of the Church in Palestine. This would doubtless provide him with quite a lot of material that he later embodied in the first twelve chapters of *Acts*. It should be noted in this respect that the speeches contained in those chapters are rather cruder in respect to their Greek than other parts of *Acts*, and this might well be due to the fact that Luke had found them in writing at Caesarea in the form of a translation into Greek from the original Aramaic in which they were spoken in the first place.

After a subsequent hearing by King Agrippa, Paul, with other prisoners, was sent to Rome in charge of Julius. Aristarchus and Luke accompanied Paul on the voyage. They journeyed round the north of Cyprus and on to Crete. On leaving here they were caught in a severe storm and for fourteen days were driven before it. The next day the ship was driven aground on Malta and broken up by the surf. All the passengers were providentially saved. After waiting three months another ship picked them up and brought them to Sicily and on to Puteoli in Italy. Here Paul 60 was met by some of the brethren and journeyed on by land *via* Appii Forum (where some more Christians met him to encourage him) to Rome. Paul was kept under guard here for two years in his own hired dwelling, and was allowed to receive visitors and speak with them concerning the faith. On this optimistic note the book of *Acts* ends.

During his imprisonment Paul wrote four letters.[1] 60–62 *Ephesians* and *Colossians* are similar in subject matter and are usually grouped together, and *Philemon* seems to have been written at about the same time, as the personal greetings in that letter are similar to those in Colossians. Paul's *Epistle to the Philippians* was probably the last of the four to be written as he appears optimistic about visiting their city soon (*Philipp.* II.24, "But I trust in the Lord that I myself also shall come shortly"). In *Ephesians* Paul writes of God's redeeming purpose in sending Jesus Christ into the world,

[1] But see above, pp. 16, 17.

c

and emphasises the great privilege of being a Christian.
This leads him in *Eph.* IV–VI to give practical exhorta-
tions regarding the way a Christian should live. Here,
as so often in Paul, the doctrinal and practical go hand
in hand. As regards Colossae, a difficult situation had
arisen there, as Christians were being lured away from

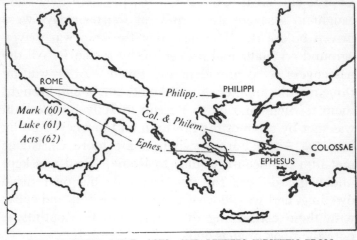

FIG. 4: MARK, LUKE, ACTS, AND LETTERS WRITTEN FROM
ROME DURING PAUL'S IMPRISONMENT (60–2)

the simple Gospel that had first been preached to them.
False teachers were trying to impose on them philo-
sophical theories that were alien to the Christian faith.
They taught that matter was evil and that asceticism
should therefore be practised. Moreover, they maintained that men must win the support of the unseen
spiritual powers by worshipping them. All this led
Paul to stress the fact that Christ had actually created
the material world (1.16, "In Him were all things
created, in the heavens and upon the earth, things

visible and things invisible") and that He was the all
sufficient Saviour of men (II.9, "In Him dwelleth *all*
the fulness of the Godhead bodily"). The short
Epistle to Philemon was written by Paul to the Christian
of that name who lived at Colossae. Philemon's slave
Onesimus had run away from him and had somehow
come under Paul's influence. He was converted and
requested by Paul to return to his master. The letter
was a plea to Philemon to treat Onesimus leniently.
Philippians is one of the warmest of Paul's letters, for
the Christians there meant a great deal to him; "I
thank my God upon all my remembrance of you" he
says in 1.3. The note of joy resounds through the
whole letter—the sheer joy of being a Christian.

Already some of the leaders of the Church had met
their death and the lives of others—like Paul—were in
jeopardy. There was a real need now that more
adequate written accounts of our Lord's life and
teaching should be made. True, there were lists of
sayings of our Lord in existence (*Q* being among them)
and lists of *testimonia* were in circulation, but these
were hardly sufficient in view of the serious situation
confronting the Church. MARK, who was in Rome 60
at this time (*Col.* IV.10), supplied this vital need.
According to the ancient writer Papias, MARK had
been Peter's companion and whilst listening to Peter's
addresses had taken notes. From these he composed
the *Gospel* which bears his name. Besides what Peter
told him, Mark probably included in his *Gospel* sayings
of Jesus, parables, and events that he had heard or
read about elsewhere. Many of these would naturally
be "common property" in the Church, and Mark

would find them useful. Professor C. H. Dodd has pointed out (in *The Apostolic Preaching and its Development*) that Mark's *Gospel* is an elaboration on a grand scale of the facts that the early preachers presented in

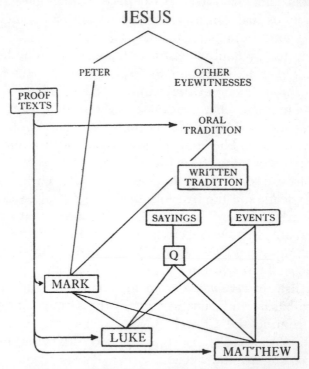

FIG. 5: STRUCTURE OF THE SYNOPTIC GOSPELS

summary form in their sermons. Jerome tells us that it was approved by Peter before publication.

While in Rome, Luke felt the need for an account to be written of the rise of Christianity and its expansion as far as Rome. This was most needful, as Paul was on trial for this very faith, and if the facts could be made plain, his chances of release would be greater. Luke had to publish his work in two volumes, owing to its length. The first deals with the history as far as the ascension of Christ, and the second volume carries on from there up to Paul's imprisonment in Rome. The first volume appears in our Bible under LUKE's name, and we find that in compiling it he did not only use his own notes ("*Proto-Luke*"), but also the newly published *Gospel according to St Mark* which gave him additional material. The second volume is *The Acts of the Apostles*,[1] and its apologetic tone and high opinion of Roman Law and customs is probably to be accounted for by the circumstances attending its writing. Luke had already collected quite a lot of information for the early chapters of this second volume from his contacts with Christians in various places (see above, p. 22). In compiling the account of Paul's journeys he would have his own diary and memory to fall back on besides being able to converse with the Apostle Paul himself about his missionary activities. Luke does not tell us the outcome of Paul's trial, but apparently he was released. Those who date the book later are faced with the difficulty of explaining why Luke did not mention Paul's release and other important events which occurred subsequently. The fact that Luke shows no trace of having read Paul's epistles (which circulated very early in the Church's history) is a strong argument in favour of the earlier dating. For an able defence of this date see the commentaries on *Acts* by F. F. Bruce.

The Muratorian Fragment (about A.D. 180) states

---

[1] But see below, p. 34.

that Paul then undertook missionary work in Spain.
There is no other direct evidence for this except that
in writing to the Romans before his imprisonment
(*Rom.* xv.24, 28), he mentions a proposed visit to that
62–4 country.   It is clear from *I Timothy* and *Titus*,[1]
however, that Paul undertook further missionary work
in the east after his release, as we learn from *I Tim.* 1.3,
that he left Timothy in charge at Ephesus after a visit
there, and Titus in charge in Crete (*Tit.* 1.5).   These
two letters give instructions on church-government
and the moral qualifications of Church officers.

63   It was about this time that JUDE the Lord's brother
wrote his short tract condemning false teachers.

[Some date the *Epistle of James* in this period, holding
that he was acquainted with some of Paul's epistles (see above,
p. 9).]

This time of comparative quiet was soon broken by
a new outbreak of persecution directed by the Emperor
Nero against the Christians.   Paul was again imprisoned
in Rome and realising that he was a condemned man
wrote his last instructions to Timothy in what we
64 know as the *Second Epistle to Timothy*.   He exhorted
this younger warrior faithfully to fulfil his duties as
a minister of Jesus Christ and to defend the truth of
the Gospel.   Soon after he had written this letter Paul
met a martyr's death.

At about this time Peter was also imprisoned and
wrote a letter of encouragement to the Christians of
Asia Minor.   Apparently organised persecution had
not yet reached that part of the world, but PETER

[1] But see below, p. 34.

wrote his *First Epistle* in order that when the storm 64
broke they would be prepared spiritually. Besides
dealing with suffering for the sake of righteousness, he
reminds them in very moving words of the cost of their
redemption and the duty of all Christians to maintain
a high moral standard in their lives.

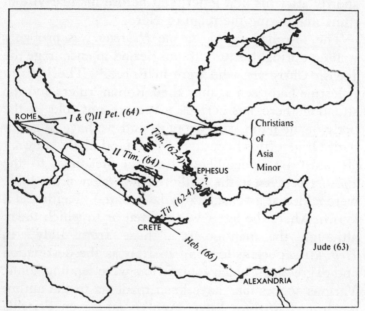

ROME

I & (?)II Pet. (64)

Christians
of
Asia
Minor

? I Tim. (62-4)

II Tim. (64)

EPHESUS

?

Tit (62-4)

CRETE

Heb. (66)

Jude (63)

ALEXANDRIA

FIG. 6: LETTERS WRITTEN 62–6

Many scholars dispute the view that Peter wrote the 64
second letter[1] which bears his name in our New
Testament. This is largely due to the fact that
II Peter shows considerable dependence on the *Epistle
of Jude*, to which some scholars assign a date later than
Peter's death. Also there are indications in *II Peter*

[1] See below, p. 34.

that it was written late on in the first century, or even
in the second (*e.g.* it implies that Paul's epistles had
already been collected and were regarded as Scripture
—*II Pet*. III.15, 16). Neither is there any definite
mention of the letter by early writers until Origen
(A.D. 230). If Peter wrote it, he must have done so
shortly after his first letter, and before his martyrdom
sometime during the reign of Nero.

66   The so-called *Epistle to the Hebrews* was probably
written during this tumultuous period to encourage the
Jewish Christians who were in Rome.[1] The Jews in
Palestine had risen against their Roman rulers and the
situation there was serious. We are not told in the
body of the letter who wrote it, and we have to admit
with Origen (third century) "that God alone knows."
(It must be remembered that the headings to the
Epistles as given in the Authorised Version of the Bible
were added at a considerably later date.) Neither is it
known where the letter was written or to which town,
although the mention of "those from Italy" in
Heb. XIII.24 seems to point to Italy as the destination
and to greetings which compatriots were sending home.
Various suggestions have been made as to the author
(such as Barnabas, Luke, Apollos and even Priscilla
and Aquila—a suggestion of Harnack which seems
quite probable) and as to the place of origin (Alexandria
probably being the best owing to the "Alexandrian"

---

[1] W. Manson in *The Epistle to the Hebrews* (1951), suggests that
the letter was written to encourage Jewish Christians to break
away from their traditional ritual and to realise the world mission
of Christianity. He thinks that the writer was of the same spiritual
stock as Stephen the Martyr, who appreciated more than most the
universality of the new Faith.

colouring of the letter). The question is still not settled whether the recipients were Jews or Gentiles, but in view of the Jewish character of the letter and its frequent appeal to the Old Testament the former seems the more probable. Various facts derived from the letter count against the Pauline authorship. The style and vocabulary are so unlike the Apostle's, and this type of writing—a long sustained parallel with the Old Testament—is certainly not found in any of his letters. The writer seems to have a different outlook from Paul on faith and the Old Testament Law. The fact that the Church in the West did not recognise it until the fourth century tells considerably against Apostolic authorship.

But what treasures there are in this book! Here Christ the mediator of the New Covenant is extolled and his high priesthood set forth in awe-inspiring terms. The Old Covenant is replaced by the New "in his blood," and behold all things are become new. The author is just overwhelmed with his transcendent theme.

During this period from A.D. 55 to A.D. 66 the outlook for the Church had changed considerably. The era of persecutions had begun and already some of the Church's greatest leaders—Paul, Peter, and James for example—had been martyred. But their written word remained to inspire future generations, and soon another, equally as great as they were, was to take up the pen, and like them to make the whole world his debtor; that man was the Apostle John.

CHAPTER IV

THE CLOSE OF THE APOSTOLIC AGE

THE year A.D. 70 was a fateful one for the Jews, because in it the Roman general Titus (the son of the Emperor Vespasian) captured Jerusalem, slaying thousands of Jews and taking captive thousands more. This national catastrophe came as a severe blow to Jewish Christians, as Messianic expectations were closely connected with the Holy City in the minds of the Jews. Was Jesus really the Messiah after all? The question was bound 70–80 to be in the mind of many. MATTHEW wrote his *Gospel* in order to substantiate this supreme claim that the Church made for Jesus. He shows Christianity as the consummation of the Jewish faith and Jesus as the long-awaited Messiah. To prove his point Matthew makes abundant use of *testimonia*. What is more, Jesus will come again and He shall be Lord of all. This point is emphasised because already men were asking "where is the promise of His coming?" and there was need for waning hopes to be revived. In the meantime men should recognise the Church as the New Israel, built upon faith in Christ (*Mt*. XVI.18) and having power to arbitrate in disputes (XVIII.17).

In compiling his *Gospel*, Matthew made use of Mark's, but he seems to have had access to other material which neither Mark or Luke knew or used.

This matter which is peculiar to Matthew is referred to as *M* and includes nativity stories and additional facts about the last days of our Lord's life. Thus we see that Luke's words at the opening of his *Gospel* are quite true—"many had taken in hand to draw up a narrative"—and Matthew, like Luke, did not hesitate to use this earlier material.

These were troublous times for Christianity. The Emperor Domitian who ruled the Roman Empire from A.D. 81 to A.D. 96 was far from sympathetic towards the Christians. He persecuted believers not only in Rome but also in Asia. Within the Church there was considerable falling away in some quarters. There was thus urgent need for a solemn warning to be issued to back-sliders, but at the same time a word of encouragement to the faithful assuring them that Christ was still on the throne in spite of the arrogance of Imperial Rome. In these circumstances the *Book of Revelation* was written by the aged Apostle John, a book admirably 81–96 fulfilling this dual purpose. (Some think that another John wrote this book.)

Somewhat late in this period John wrote his homily on fellowship with God, the so-called *I John*, a book which reminds us so much by its tone of the Fourth *Gospel*. *II John* followed, and was probably written by the same author, although it should be noticed that the writer styles himself "the elder" (vs. 1). The letter is addressed to the "elect lady," which might refer to a woman, but more likely to a church with which John was acquainted. *III John* was written to a man named Gaius, a leader in some church. Both these letters are pastoral in character.

94-100   [Some scholars would date the *Acts of the Apostles* about this time, on the assumption that the author had read a work of Josephus published about A.D. 94. The evidence for Luke's acquaintance with this book, however, is far from conclusive (see above, p. 27).]

90-100   JOHN, "the beloved Apostle," was now an old man. As he reflected on the days now long past when he had walked with Jesus in Galilee, and as he meditated on all that Christ had meant to him in the long years that had intervened, he was filled with a deep longing that others should believe on this One whom "to know was life eternal." He called for one to write down his memoirs, he himself bearing witness to the facts recorded. "This is the disciple which beareth witness of these things, and wrote [or 'caused to write'] these things: and we know that his witness is true" (*Jn.* XXI.24). It was the gospel of the love of God written out of love for men. "These are written, that ye may believe that Jesus is the Christ, the son of God; and that believing ye may have life in his name."

Could not the same reason be given for the writing of all the other New Testament books? They too were written that men might believe on Jesus Christ, and their message comes down the centuries to us to-day appealing to us to put our faith in him. How these documents were preserved and transmitted to us it is the purpose of the following pages to show.

[It should be noted that many question the Petrine authorship of *II Peter* and place it at the beginning of the second century (see above, p. 29).

Some would also date the Pastoral Epistles (*I* and *II Timothy*, and *Titus*) in this period, on the grounds that they reflect a form of Church-government later than the days of the Apostle Paul. Arguments from the non-Pauline character of the vocabulary and style are also put forward in support of this date, besides the contention that key-notes of Paul's doctrine such as the fatherhood of God, and the life in Christ are lacking (see above, p. 28).]

CHAPTER V

SPREADING THE NEWS

IN the preceding pages we have traced when and where the New Testament books were written, and have observed that the recipients dwelt in many different places scattered over the Mediterranean area. What happened to these original letters of the Apostles and others? We can be sure that they were treasured by the churches which received them, and were shown to Christians from other towns who might visit them. For example, a Christian merchant in the course of his voyages might put in at the harbour near to Corinth. Being shown the letters which Paul had written to that Church he would realise that they contained teaching which would be invaluable to his own church at Rome or wherever it might be, and would make a rough copy of it. Thus in due course the Church at Rome would not only have the letter which Paul wrote to it but also those written to Corinth. In this way groups of books would be built up in important centres of the faith. Others who came to Rome would be interested in these epistles which had originally been written to the Corinthian Christians and would make a copy of the copy, and this process of copying would go on all over the then known world, wherever the sacred writings were to be found. Now two important facts should be noted about these early copies. First, they were often made by ordinary people and not by professional scribes. This meant that the likelihood of copyists' errors creeping into the text was great. Secondly, the copies were made for edification, and so slight altera- tion of phrasing or even the omission of an unimportant word would not be considered of any consequence. Thus a whole variety of slightly different readings of the epistles (etc.) came into being. But the wording of the text as it existed at some great centre such as Rome, however, would obviously have great prestige, and owing to the availability of scribes in such places would tend to be multiplied much more than a form of the text preserved in some remote town. Thus around some of the important cities of the Roman Empire a certain more or less fixed form of the text came into being, and this is referred to as "a local text" of that particular town. More will be said about this later.

Many of these ancient copies of the Greek Testament have come down to us. Greek was the "universal language" of the Roman Empire, and as the Church spread, copies of the Greek text were in great demand. But the need was also felt for the translation of the New Testament into other tongues such as Latin and Syriac, and copies of these various versions have also come down to us. Very soon large numbers of books were written by Christian men and inevitably these often quoted from the New Testament. Since copies of many of these books have also been preserved, they also furnish us with the means of determining the exact wording of the Sacred Text.

Let us take a quick glance at some of the very

Date	Kind of Writing	GREEK MSS.	ANCIENT VSS.	FATHERS	Date
100	U N C I A L W R I T I N G I N U S E				100
		John Rylands Fragm.	Tatian's *Diatessaron*	Irenaeus	
200		Pap. Bodmer II	Old Latin Old Syriac	Origen	200
		Chester Beatty Papp.	Egyptian	Cyprian	
300		Oxyrhyncus Papp.		Lucian Eusebius	300
		B ℵ			
			Latin Vulgate		
400		A C D	Syriac Peshitta	Cyril of Alexandria	400
500		W			500
		Purple MSS. ΣΝΟΦ	Georgian		
600					600
700					700
	M I N U S C U L E W R I T I N G	L			
800		Θ			800
900		33 565			900
1000		28			1000
1100		700 1			1100
1200		13			1200

FIG. 7: LEADING AUTHORITIES FOR THE TEXT OF THE
NEW TESTAMENT

earliest evidence for our New Testament. The oldest Greek manuscript of the Greek text in existence is known as the John Rylands Papyrus. It is a very small **150** fragment of the *Gospel according to St John* XVIII.31–3, 37–8, and is dated about A.D. 150. Not long after this manuscript was written a harmony of the four *Gospels* was published by an Assyrian Christian called TATIAN. It is not certain whether he wrote this work in Greek or Syriac, but it was undertaken while he was in Rome and therefore reflects the type of text current in that part of the world. This work—known as *Tatian's* **170** *Diatessaron*—was completed about A.D. 170. Unfortunately it only exists in translation (Latin, Dutch, Armenian, and Arabic), apart from a very small Greek fragment discovered at Dura in Mesopotamia, and as already remarked this also may not be the original language in which the *Diatessaron* was written.

Before the end of the century, IRENAEUS, the Bishop **185** of Lyons, had written his important work entitled *Against Heresies*, which furnishes us in its quotations with evidence for the New Testament.

During the first half of the third century, three very important translations were made of the New Testament. They are the LATIN, the SYRIAC, and the **200–50** EGYPTIAN. The first evidence for a Latin translation comes from North Africa, and those Latin MSS which preserve this African type of Latin text are the best Latin MSS, especially the two denoted by the letters k (*Codex Bobiensis*, 4th–5th cent.) and e (*Codex Palatinus*, 5th cent.). The best representatives of the European Latin text are b (*Codex Veronensis*, 5th cent.) and a (*Codex Vercellensis*, 4th cent.). The origin of these

D

old Latin texts is unknown and the relation of each to the other is a complicated matter, but they are invaluable for the re-construction of the original text. TERTULLIAN (*c.* 150–220), who wrote in Africa, used the Latin text, as also did CYPRIAN (*c.* 200–58), Bishop of Carthage.

The Old Syriac Version is also to be dated during this period. The most important MS of this version is known as the Sinaitic Syriac MS (4th cent.) discovered by two Cambridge ladies, Mrs Lewis and Mrs Gibson, in 1892. Previous to this discovery the Old Syriac was read in the Curetonian Syriac MS (5th cent.). This is similar to the Sinaitic MS, but differs from it in considerable detail and does not appear to be so trustworthy. Both MSS contain the Gospels only.

Many manuscripts exist of the other important translation made during the first half of the third century—the Egyptian or Coptic Version. This is found in two forms. The better text, which originated in Upper Egypt near the source of the Nile, is known as the Sahidic text. The other form—the Bohairic—originated in the Nile Delta around Alexandria. It was in this great city that the famous scholar ORIGEN spent much of his life and published important Christian literature. The quotations of Origen are of great value in the determination of the text, and his various works include commentaries on the New Testament books.

In 1956 the discovery of another ancient Greek manuscript was announced—Papyrus Bodmer II (𝔭66). This codex is dated about 200, and the surviving part contains *Jn.* I.1–VI.11, VI.35–XIV.26.

It is in a good state of preservation, and shows clearly the ancient method of book-production. Though the scribe was somewhat careless, it affords valuable evidence as to the text of *John* at this early date.[1]

But by far the most important witness to the New Testament which comes to us from the third century is the group of three manuscripts discovered by Mr Chester Beatty, and known as the Chester Beatty Papyri. The fragments include portions of all four *Gospels* and the *Acts* (contained in Papyrus 45, as it is 200–50 called), parts of *Romans*, *Philippians*, *Colossians*, and *I Thessalonians* (in Papyrus 46), together with ten leaves 200–50 of the *Book of Revelation* (Papyrus 47). These papyri 250–300 are valuable witnesses to the New Testament writings and show how little the text of the New Testament has suffered from scribal copying throughout the long years. The discovery was announced in 1931.

From this early period twenty-one other papyrus fragments (mostly very small) have survived. They were discovered with nine other fragments of later date at Oxyrhyncus in Egypt. Although small, they do however help us to see the form that the New Testament took at that early date.

The foregoing will have given some indication of the great amount of material we have at our disposal from which to construct the New Testament as it existed in the very earliest centuries of our era. But many other first-class witnesses to the text have yet to be considered, as will be seen from the next chapter.

[1] See V. Martin, *Pap. Bodmer II*, Bibl. Bodmer, 1956.

CHAPTER VI

THE TEXT OF THE NEW TESTAMENT
FIXED AND MULTIPLIED

DURING the course of our discussions we have had
frequent cause to refer to corruptions[1] in the text of
MSS, and it may be well at this point to ask ourselves
how these occur and what forms they take. Most
corruptions in the text of MSS are unintentional, and
may be grouped as follows.

1. DITTOGRAPHY—the accidental repetition of a letter
   or group of letters. This was very easily done
   as uncial MSS (*i.e.* those written in capital letters)
   were written with no division between the words.

2. HAPLOGRAPHY—the opposite error, *i.e.* the writing
   of a letter or group once when it ought to be
   repeated. As an example of this see the Greek
   text of *I Thess.* II.7, where some MSS read
   ETENHΘHMENHΠIOI ("we were gentle"),
   and others ETENHΘHMENNHΠIOI ("we were
   babes"). The only difference is the repetition of
   the letter N. Only the context can enable us to
   decide which is correct in such cases, when the
   MS evidence is equally divided.

[1] In this section I am particularly indebted to Kirsopp Lake,
The Text of the New Testament (Rivingtons). See also L. Vaganay,
Introduction to the Textual Criticism of the New Testament.

3. HOMOIOTELEUTON—the confusion of words ending in similar syllables. This often leads to the omission of a complete line or lines of the MS that is being copied. For example in *Jn.* VI.11, some MSS expand the verse and read:

. . . ΔΙΕΔѠΚΕ	. . . He distributed
ΤΟΙϹ[ΜΑΘΗΤΑΙϹ	to the [disciples
ΟΙΔΕΜΑΘΗΤΑΙ	and the disciples
ΤΟΙϹ]ΑΝΑΚΕΙΜ	to them] that were set
ΕΝΟΙϹ . . .	down. . . .

Compare the A.V. and R.V. here. Did the eye of an early scribe jump from the first ΤΟΙϹ to the second and hence some MSS have the abbreviated form of the verse?[1]

4. ITACISM—the accidental alteration of a vowel owing to similarity of sound. The awkward reading in *Rom.* V.1, "let us have (ΕΧѠΜΕΝ) peace with God" may be due to a scribe writing the Greek letter Ѡ instead of Ο. ΕΧΟΜΕΝ would give the much easier reading "we have peace wtih God."

Besides these causes a scribe might easily misread a word, or make a mistake in reading an abbreviation. (Abbreviations are a regular feature in Greek and Latin MSS.)

The following reasons can be given for intentional alterations in MSS:

[1] From Burgon and Miller, *Causes of Corruption in the traditional Text* (1896), p. 37.

1. If the scribe knows that in another translation with which he is familiar a text runs somewhat differently, he may introduce this other rendering into his MS.

2. If he is accustomed to hearing texts quoted in the liturgy of his own church rather differently from the form in front of him he may prefer it to copying the MS. Thus the insertion in some MSS of *Acts* VIII.37, which many important MSS omit, may be due to its creeping in from some well-known formula that baptismal candidates were expected to utter at their baptism.

3. The scribe may assimilate one gospel narrative which he is copying to another, *e.g.* when copying Luke's account of the feeding of the five thousand, he may insert interesting details from Mark.

4. He may alter a text to agree with his theology. This is a very rare form of corruption, but was definitely employed by Marcion, a heretic.

Thus from the very earliest times there was a very great variety of different readings of the text in existence. Early in the fourth century a certain scholar named LUCIAN carefully compared different readings of the New Testament with which he was acquainted and produced a revised form of the text. This "revised text" soon became very popular, not only at Antioch, where Lucian worked, but also at Constantinople, and, before long, all over the Mediterranean area. Since it soon became the dominant form of the New Testament in the Byzantine Empire, this revised text is usually referred to as the Byzantine text. Later Greek Manuscripts mostly contain this late form of the text, and are therefore of negligible value in determining the original wording of the New Testament. When the New Testament was first printed in the sixteenth century, it was largely based upon inferior manuscripts of this revised type, and our Authorised Version was also largely a translation from manuscripts of this class: hence it is far less valuable for purposes of Bible-study than the Revised Version, which is based on much better manuscripts.

Later in the fourth century, Pope Damasus of Rome became disturbed by the great variety of different readings of the Latin New Testament which were in existence, and took steps to have a revised form of the Latin Text produced. This work was put into the hands of JEROME, who published his "revised Latin text," known as the (Latin) VULGATE, about the year A.D. 391. He used not only Latin manuscripts but also 391 Greek ones for this task. Many copies of the Vulgate have come down to us, some early and some later in date.

Shortly after this another revised text was published, this time in Syriac. It differs considerably from the Old Syriac mentioned earlier and reveals the fact that Rabbula, who undertook the work, had consulted Greek manuscripts of the revised type. This revised Syriac is known as the PESHITTA and is dated 411 A.D. 411.

In spite of these revisions, a large number of early manuscripts which have survived still contain early forms of the text, although they were not copied until after A.D. 311. Some of these very valuable manuscripts of the Greek text will now be listed.

All the Greek MSS mentioned so far are written on papyrus, as that was the common writing material used until the fourth century; but at that time vellum was substituted for papyrus in book-production. Vellum was made from the skins of animals, and was far more durable than papyrus, which was manufactured from the fibrous pith of a form of water reed.

300–400   Perhaps the most famous of all vellum MSS is the *Codex Sinaiticus*, made in the fourth century and discovered by Tischendorf in 1859. The manuscript is written in four columns and has been subjected to alteration by scribes since its first writing. The manuscript is now in the British Museum and is referred to by the Hebrew letter 'aleph (ℵ). This MS belongs to the type known as the Alexandrian family— a form of the text most prevalent around Alexandria.

The *Codex Vaticanus* (B) is of about the same date as the Sinaiticus, and belongs to the same family. It is written in three columns and is at present in the Vatican Library. This MS was greatly valued by Westcott and Hort (two of the leading scholars behind the English R.V.) who considered it to be unrivalled in the purity of its text. The Sinaiticus contains the whole of the New Testament, but the Vaticanus lacks *Heb.* IX.14–28, *I* and *II Timothy*, *Titus* and *Philemon*.

400–500   To the early fifth century belongs the *Codex Alexandrinus* (A), now in the British Museum. This MS also belongs to the Alexandrian family of MSS except in the *Gospels*, where its text is somewhat inferior. It contains both Testaments almost complete.   Three scribes took part in the writing of the New Testament, and several correctors worked on the MS subsequently. Later in the century another MS belonging to this family was produced, the *Codex Ephraemi*, but it is not as valuable as the great MSS ℵ and B.   This *Codex Ephraemi* (C) is interesting in that it is a palimpsest, *i.e.* the original Greek was partly obliterated and a Greek translation of a work by the early Syrian Father Ephraim written over it in the twelfth century.

The *Codex Bezae* (D), another MS of this century, is notable for its tendency to expand the text, besides presenting many minor differences from the majority of MSS. (For example to *Lk*. XXIII.53, it adds the fact that hardly twenty men could roll away the stone. There is a long insertion about a man working on the Sabbath, at *Lk*. VI.4.) This MS belongs to the Western Family[1] (European branch), and is now in the University Library at Cambridge.

The Washington MS (W), also of the fifth century, was acquired in 1906 by Charles L. Freer of Detroit. It is unusual in that four different types of text are to be found in it. Kenyon thinks that the varieties of text used point to the MS having been produced in a library, or having descended from a MS so produced. This MS only contains the *Gospels*.

From the sixth century four beautiful "purple vellum" MSS have come down to us. They contain portions of the four *Gospels*, and are denoted by the symbols Σ,N,O,Φ. The Georgian Version—a translation made from the Armenian—also belongs to this

500–600

---

[1] See below, p. 54.

century, and has been shown of recent years to be of considerable value.

700–800 The *Codex Regius* (L) of the *Gospels* belongs to the seventh century. It belongs to the Alexandrian family, and is now in the National Library of Paris.

800–900 To the next century belongs the *Codex Koridethi* of the *Gospels*. This MS is very roughly written, but it is an important representative of the Caesarean Family. It is denoted by the Greek letter theta (Θ).

All the manuscripts described so far are written in capital letters and are known as uncial manuscripts. About the year A.D. 800, however, a form of Greek writing similar to our own "running hand" began to be used in copying MSS, although the old uncial writing was still used by some copyists until about A.D. 1000. This running hand was called minuscule writing. As a general rule, then, an uncial MS is more accurate, since it is usually older than the minuscule, and so has probably been copied less, *i.e.* it has fewer "ancestors." On the other hand, however, the following points must be borne in mind:

1. Some minuscules are just as old as some uncials.

2. Although generally later, minuscules may preserve old, correct renderings of the text, and be far superior to an uncial that is much older; for example, Min. 33 is very important, although of 800–900 the ninth century. It is similar to the Vaticanus and the Sinaiticus, two of our best uncial MSS.

3. The most important thing is not the date of a MS but its pedigree, *i.e.* the quality of the MSS which form its ancestors. Thus a comparatively late

minuscule MS may have been copied from a very good early MS and so be of very great value. Such a good pedigree would make it far superior to an older MS that had been made from a very corrupt copy.

The following are just a few of the most important minuscules. They are denoted by numbers, as opposed to the capital letters which are used for uncials. From the ninth or tenth century, we have Min. 565 800–1000 written in gold letters on purple vellum. Min. 28 is dated in the eleventh century, whereas Mins. 1, 13 1000–1100 and 700 all belong to the twelfth. More will be said 1100–1200 later about these important MSS.

The invention of printing in the fifteenth century completely revolutionised the task of copying the New Testament, for it now became possible, once the type had been set up, to make thousands of accurate copies of the sacred text without any fears of scribal errors creeping in. Early in the year 1456 the first printed 1456 Bible was issued in Germany. It was a copy of the Latin Vulgate Version, and is known as the Gutenberg or Mazarin Bible. The first printed Greek New Testament (prepared by Erasmus) was published in 1516 1516. (This was based mainly on Mins. 1 and 2.) An English translation of this appeared ten years later in 1526, and was the work of TYNDALE. Various translations followed, until eventually in 1611 the English AUTHORISED VERSION (A.V.) was published by com- 1611 mand of King James VI & I. Scholars, however, were not satisfied with the Greek text from which this translation was made. They carefully examined the

MSS which they had and tried by scientific methods to ascertain the exact words of the New Testament writers. This study is known as textual criticism, and more will be said about it in the next chapter. After generations of hard work in this field by many scholars, it was finally decided to undertake a Revised Version of the Bible. Committees were set up both in this country and in America to carry out this purpose. All the best Greek MSS, versions in other languages, and quotations of the Scriptures from ancient sources were carefully examined in preparing the Greek text from 1881 which the translation was to be made. The REVISED VERSION (R.V.) of the New Testament was published in 1881 and that of the Old Testament followed four years later.

Modern versions of the Scriptures now followed in 1901 quick succession. In 1901 the AMERICAN STANDARD VERSION (A.S.V.) was published. This was simply the English Revised Version modified in accordance with the recommendations that had been made by the American Committee when working on the Revised Version. The Weymouth New Testament, Twentieth Century New Testament, and Moffatt's translation appeared in the next two decades. In 1930 a revision of the American Standard Version was put in hand, 1946 with the result that the (American) REVISED STANDARD VERSION (R.S.V.) was published in 1946. This translation took full cognisance of the latest MS evidence, and the advances that had been made in understanding the Greek in which the New Testament was written. Special care was taken that the translation should convey accurately the message of the sacred

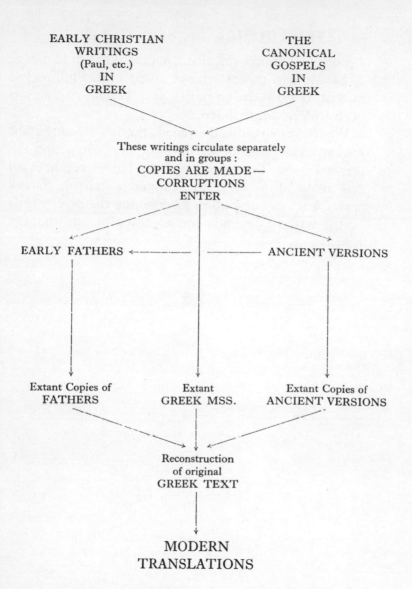

FIG. 8: TRANSMISSION OF THE TEXT OF THE NEW TESTAMENT

writers, and, moreover, that it should do so in language of beauty and power. Since 1946, J. B. Phillips has published a translation of the New Testament that has been widely commended.

We have already discussed the most important ancient evidence that we have for re-constructing the original New Testament; we must now see how all this material is used to produce a reliable Greek text, for upon our skill in ascertaining the exact words of the writers depends the accuracy of any modern translation.

CHAPTER VII

RECOVERING THE LOST ORIGINAL

CONFRONTED by such a mass of evidence for our New Testament one might well be bewildered, and wonder how the exact wording of the original can possibly be arrived at amid so many variant readings, both small and great. If we try to reconstruct the history of these variations we shall see that the position is not so hopeless as it all seems at first sight.[1]

By the end of the third century many copies of parts of the New Testament in various languages were in circulation over the then known world. Owing to difficulties of transcription these all differed slightly from one another, but they tended to fall into different families, each family having its own particular characteristics. Thus around Alexandria an Alexandrian type of text would gradually be built up, around Caesarea a Caesarean type, and so on. For example, the Western family of MSS (represented by the Greek MS D and the Old Latin MS e) differs in its wording of *Lk*. v.10 f. When a MS is discovered, its family has to be ascertained by noting whether it has readings characteristic of this or that family. Very often a MS is of mixed descent, for example it may have been

---

[1] See Map 2 (at the end of the book).

made by a scribe copying from a Western type MS, but occasionally referring to an Alexandrian type, with the result that it embodies a mixture of Western and Alexandrian elements.

From the fourth century as we have seen, a standard type of text emerges—the Byzantine Text (also called the RECEIVED TEXT or *Textus receptus*). This quickly replaced the earlier types, and earlier MSS were often revised to accord with it. The majority of Greek MSS in existence are of the Byzantine type. Being late, they are far inferior to the few MSS which preserve pre-Byzantine types of text. The Authorised Version was largely made from Byzantine-type MSS, and hence it suffers from all their defects.

In seeking to discover the actual wording of the original we can place on one side the great number of Greek and other MSS which preserve this late type of text. What about the Greek MSS, versions, and Fathers which however have the old readings? These are divided up into five families which are centred at the places from which their name is taken.

For example, the ALEXANDRIAN text sprang up around Alexandria, and is best represented in B (*codex Vaticanus*) and ℵ (*codex Sinaiticus*).

As we move westwards from Alexandria we come to Carthage in North Africa. This NORTH AFRICAN family includes the Old Latin MSS k and e.

Across the Mediterranean we arrive at Italy and Gaul, whose type of New Testament is seen in D (*codex Bezae*) and the Old Latin MSS b and a. Kenyon groups this family with the preceding one under the general title of WESTERN TEXT.

Moving to the east of the Mediterranean we arrive at Antioch in Syria. The type of text that was used here is preserved particularly in the Sinaitic Syriac and the Curetonian Syriac. This ANTIOCHIAN family[1] was classed with the two preceding families under one general heading of Western Family by the great nineteenth-century scholars Westcott and Hort, but subsequent study has shown that two separate groups must be recognised.

The discovery of the last family—the CAESAREAN—was the work of Dr Streeter, who put the finishing touches to the work of other scholars. W. H. Ferrar had found that four minuscules, of which Min. 13 was one, formed an independent group which he called Family 13. Eight other minuscules were subsequently added to the family. Another scholar named Kirsopp Lake then discovered that Min. 1 could be grouped with eight other minuscules to form Family 1. An important stage was reached in the definition of the Caesarean family when it was found that the uncial codex Θ (the Koridethi MS, probably of the eighth century) could be grouped along with Families 1 and 13. Dr Streeter then devoted his attention to a study of the Early Father Origen (born late second century) and found that the type of text represented by Families 1 and 13 was used in part by Origen at that early date. So another ancient type of text had been discovered. Other manuscripts were later added to the family (notably 28, 565, 700 and part of Codex W), besides the four beautiful purple-vellum manuscripts

[1] Or SYRIAC TEXT.

of the sixth century N,Σ,O,Φ, and the Georgian Version.[1]

These then are the five main families into which our manuscripts, versions, and quotations from the Fathers can be divided. Map 2 shows the location of these families along the coasts of the Mediterranean, according to Dr Streeter's theory of "local texts." In each case the primary and secondary authorities for each family are given, together with important Early Fathers who used the local text. (It will be observed that both the Alexandrian and Caesarean texts are found in Origen's writings.) It must, however, be realised that no manuscript is a pure offspring of its family; thus, though ℵ is regarded as a manuscript of Alexandrian type, it contains several readings of Western type. As regards the Chester Beatty Papyri (see Fig. 9), it will be seen that in *Mark* 𝔓45 is definitely Caesarean; in *Luke* and *John* it lies about midway between Alexandrian and Western; but in *Acts* it is markedly Alexandrian. These papyri seem to belong to a period prior to the emergence of clearly-marked families, as also does 𝔓66 (Pap. Bodmer II).

A few examples may help us to see how this theory of "local texts" enables us to recover the original wordings.

If we look at the Revised Version, we shall find that *Mt*. XVIII.11 is omitted from the text. On studying

---

[1] Dr Streeter applied the term "Caesarean Text" to this family because he maintained that Origen used it after his arrival at Caesarea from Alexandria. But recent study has shown a "Caesarean" element in Origen's writings *before* his visit to that town. As 𝔓45 (which has a distinct Caesarean text in Mark) was discovered in Egypt, it seems to furnish evidence that the Caesarean text may not have originated in Caesarea.

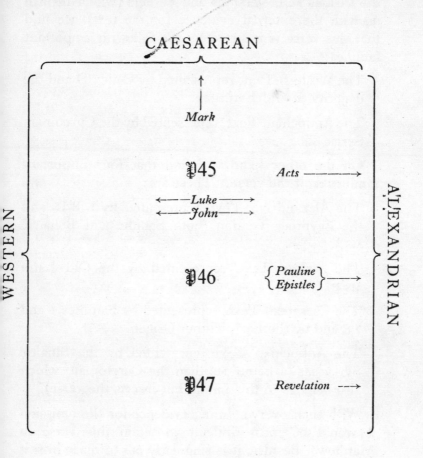

FIG. 9: THE CHESTER BEATTY PAPYRI

The 45 surviving verses of *Matthew* are so fragmentary that its
type of text cannot be determined.

the various MSS, Versions and Fathers (which furnish us with the external evidence for the text), we find that this verse is inserted by the following important families:

The Western Text, represented by Codex D and the majority of Old Latin MSS.

The Antiochian Text, represented by the Curetonian Syriac MS.

On the other hand, we find that four important families omit the verse. These are:

The Alexandrian Text, represented by א,B,L, and the Egyptian Version (both Sahidic and Bohairic MSS).

The African Text, represented by the Old Latin MS e.

The Caesarean Text, represented by Families 1 and 13, and by the Early Father Origen.

The Antiochian Text represented by the Sinaitic Syriac MS (a better MS than the Curetonian, which also belongs to this family but inserts the verse).

With such overwhelming evidence for the omission it would be most difficult to retain this verse in Matthew. Besides, it is singularly out of place in this context and appears to have been introduced from *Lk*. XIX.10.

A procedure such as this is called "weighing the evidence for a reading." This reading was easily weighed because of the number of families that attested it, but very often the variant readings are almost evenly balanced and the task of deciding which is the correct one is very difficult.

Every reading has to be decided on its own merits. We have already seen one guide as to the correct reading—the number of families which support a reading. Besides this external evidence for the text, if we look carefully at the variant readings we may be able to see which one was likely to occur through the error of an early scribe, and shall discount it accordingly. Thus it may be clear that one form of the text is due to homoioteleuton or to misunderstanding of an abbreviation. All this deliberation about the possibility of scribal error is entailed in weighing up the internal probability for the reading. There are three canons which help us in this process.

(*a*) Prefer the harder reading to an easier one (*difficilior lectio potior*). If a group of MSS gives a reading which is difficult grammatically, it is more likely to be correct, because a later scribe would *tend* to simplify a sentence, not make it more difficult. On the other hand, however, the more difficult reading may not be the original one; it may have arisen because the scribe's Greek was poor, and he did not realise the error he had made, so the canon has to be used with discretion.

(*b*) Prefer the shorter reading (*brevior lectio probabilior*). Some scholars such as Dr Streeter do not regard this canon favourably. The commonest error in the copying of classical Greek MSS was accidental omission, hence the longer reading would appear to be more likely original. Also, it is felt that scribes would shrink from adding to the sacred text. Professor

A. C. Clark agrees with this view, saying that scribes may accidentally omit part of a verse, but do not interpolate. He therefore contends that the Western Text (which usually gives a longer form of the text) is probably primitive as opposed to a shorter form. On the other hand, there was the temptation for a scribe to expand the MS before him if he knew a further interesting detail to insert.

(c) Prefer the reading which is unlike its parallel in another *Gospel* or incident. Assimilation of accounts in separate *Gospels* is a very common occurrence.

Let us examine another variant reading found in *Jn.* XVII.11. Some MSS and Versions read "keep them in thy name (which thou hast given me) that they may be one," whereas others read, "keep through thine own name those whom thou hast given me." The first reading is strongly attested by the Alexandrian family (represented by B,ℵ,L, and the Egyptian Sahidic and Bohairic) besides the Caesarean text (Θ, Fam. 1). The second reading is only supported (apart from minor MSS and versions) by D and less important MSS of the Western Text.

So much for the external evidence regarding these variants. What of the internal evidence? If we apply canons (a) and (c) above we shall find even more support for the first reading. It is grammatically more complex than the second—*i.e.* it is a harder reading. Canon (c) also supports the reading, because the thought expressed in the words "those whom thou hast given me" occurs frequently in this chapter (see vss. 2, 6, 9, 12, 24), and the tendency of a copyist would be to make this verse similar.

The variant reading in *Mk*. III.14 will illustrate the difficulty in deciding whether a shorter reading is due to accidental omission of part of the verse, or the longer reading is not the original but results from adding to the text. The wording "And he appointed twelve that they might be with him" is attested by the following families:

> Western (D, Old Latin)
> Alexandrian (L)
> Antiochian (Sinaitic Syriac)
> Caesarean (Fam. 1, 565, 700)

Some MSS insert the words "whom he named apostles" after the word "twelve." These are:

> Alexandrian family (B, ℵ, Egyptian versions)
> Caesarean family (Θ, Fam. 13, 28)
> Western family (W)

The evidence for inserting these additional words is strong and H. B. Swete would retain them in the text. It is possible, of course, that they were accidentally omitted from the other families. The more likely explanation however is that the words have crept in from the parallel passage in *Lk*. VI.13.

Sometimes there is a conflict between external and internal evidence for a text. For example, a few MSS of Western type (notably D, b, and the Early Father Justin) read "Thou art my beloved son, this day have I begotten thee" in *Lk*. III.22. The commoner reading, "Thou art my beloved son, in thee am I well pleased," is supported by all the other families. But is the former reading, though so poorly supported, the

correct one, and has the original text been altered in
the other families to agree with Matthew and Mark?
Against this it might be argued that the Western
Text itself has been altered to agree with *Ps.* 11.7,
and that the majority of families are correct in reading
" . . . in thee am I well pleased." Dr Streeter favours
the Western reading, however, and points out in its
favour that the other families may have altered the
true Western reading because it could be quoted by
the heretics called Adoptionists in support of their
views.

The example given above will serve to emphasise
the complexity of the task confronting the textual
critic. Before a new translation of the New Testament
is attempted the translators have to decide what form
of every verse in the New Testament they are going to
accept. In most verses the reading to be adopted is
obvious from the weight of MS and other evidence, but
other verses are singularly difficult to weigh, and the
exact form of the original can only be decided after
much deliberation. The last few years have added
very much to our evidence for the New Testament and
we can look forward to yet richer finds which shall
enable us to ascertain with even more certainty that
in every detail we have the exact words of the sacred
writers. One fact of untold importance emerges from
all those investigations; no serious error has crept
into our New Testament, and they who read it rever-
ently will be led into the Truth of God's saving love
for them.

We have traced the history of our New Testament
documents from their beginnings nineteen hundred

years ago to the present day. That same Holy Spirit who prompted and directed the New Testament writers at the first has preserved the Sacred Record through the ages, and is still present to interpret its message to us to-day.

A BRIEF BIBLIOGRAPHY

(a) For Chapters 1–4

[BRUCE, F. F.], *The Acts of the Apostles* [commentary on Greek text], ed. F. F. BRUCE, London 1951.

[——— ———], *The Book of the Acts* [commentary for English readers], ed. F. F. BRUCE, London 1954.

CLOGG, F. B., An Introduction to the New Testament, London 1940.

DODD, C. H., *The Apostolic Preaching and its Developments*, London 1944.

——— ———, *According to the Scriptures*, London 1952.

HUNTER, C. F., *The New Testament: Its Writers and their Messages*, London 1937.

McNEILE, A. H., *An Introduction to the Study of the New Testament* [2nd edn., revised by C. S. C. Williams], Oxford 1953.

MANSON, T. W., *A Companion to the Bible*, Edinburgh 1939.

STREETER, B. H., *The Four Gospels*, London 1924.

TAYLOR, V., *The Gospels: A short Introduction*, London 1945.

(b) For Chapters 5–7

KENYON, SIR F., *Recent Developments in the Textual Criticism of the Greek Bible*, London 1933.

——— ———, *The Story of the Bible*, London 1936.

——— ———, *The Text of the Greek Bible*, London 1949.

LAKE, K., *The Text of the New Testament*, London 1943.

SOUTER, A., *The Text and Canon of the New Testament* [2nd edn., revised by C. S. C. Williams], London 1954.

STREETER, B. H., *The Four Gospels*, London 1924.

VAGANAY, L., *An Introduction to the Textual Criticism of the New Testament*, London 1937.

INDEX